The Curmudgeon's Guide
to Woi

By James H(
& Colin Walton

Just another seaside ı ᴗᴗ..

Once cursed with the moniker of being God's Waiting Room because of its popularity with older folk retiring to the area, Worthing's image as a typical seaside resort is well founded. This perhaps is not the best way to start an introductory guide to our home town but let's get the ugly bits out of the way first shall we?

Yes, it has a pier with a noisy amusement arcade. Yes, there are drunken youths spilling out of the pubs and clubs at the weekends, and yes, it has all the usual shops you would find in any town or city complete with the ever popular mobility scooter to dodge along the way. Much the same as anywhere else really.

This guide book is not and will never be supported by the local council or tourism department, nor will you find it amongst the usual glossy leaflets in the station or hotel foyer. This is more of a 'Did you know - read in your room because it's raining' sort of guide. You could of course sit on the seafront with the oldies reading it - just try not to blend in too much as the undertakers are stock taking.

This Cromwellian warts and all guide is just that, blunt and honest. We will tell you both the good and bad points the highs and the lows - the nitty-gritty if you like. We also need to make clear from the outset that the opinions offered are ours and ours alone, but then again this is our home town and despite its foibles, we still love it. (We just don't go out at night).

History is Boring

There is no point in bombarding you with dates long gone and the back history of early man mining flint on Cissbury Ring or Saxon encampments on Highdown Hill, there are more than enough good local history books that go to that depth. Nelson didn't see fit to pop along and grab an ice cream on his way to the Nile to get some duty free, but we have seen our fair share of kings, queens and princesses in the past.

So in brief, Worthing started life as a small fishing community. There - that didn't take long did it?

**The Curmudgeon's Guide
to Worthing**

The Pier

The Lido

The Dome

The Prom (West)

Steyne Gardens

Splash Point

Town Centre & South Street

The Guildbourne Centre

Warwick Street

Montague Street

Chapel Road

Ambrose Place

Museum & Town Hall

The Pier

Let's plonk you down on the seafront - a very good place to start - echoing the words of Mary Poppins. We have a pier; it's as long as it needs to be and stops well short of being a danger to shipping. We are of course over looking the English Channel - the M25 of the waterways. The pier has the dubious honour of having been burnt down, blown down and even blown up (we did it during the war to stop the Germans invading and putting their towels on our deck chairs). The pointed end is home to an art deco structure of the period which at the time of writing remains empty and pointless - exactly where you'd expect a thriving café or tea room.

The pier does however have a few claims to fame; it was once used in an episode of the popular TV comedy series Men Behaving Badly, as was the Connaught Corner Restaurant a local diner across the road, and a local hotel amusingly renamed 'The Groyne View'. Splash Point, at the far eastern end of the prom, or esplanade as some prefer, became a miniature golf course for filming. The hotel has since been rebuilt as modern apartments, a growing trend in Worthing.

Worthing also has the honour of hosting the annual Birdman Competition which we stole, sorry 'took over' from nearby Bognor Regis. This well attended two day summer event sees the comical and colourful attempts of the foolhardy and serious as they try to beat the world record for un-powered flight by jumping from a high pier-bound platform. Many go several feet!

Where the pier is nailed to the land sits the Pavilion Theatre. A popular venue for ageing pop groups of the sixties and seventies to perform whilst topping up their meager pensions. Joking aside, the shows are usually very good and well attended. It is also home to craft fairs, events and exhibitions.

The Lido

West of the pier you will probably spot the Lido. Lido's are famed as being outdoor swimming pools for the masses; ours hasn't actually got a pool. Apparently it's still there, but what was once an open air pool filled with seawater, has long since been paved over and is now a store room – given the state of the local seawater at times, probably a blessing.

Today at the Lido you will find entertainment for the kiddies in the shape of small fairground rides, a place for a cuppa, an ice cream and some souvenir shops.....oh as well as the obligatory amusement arcade. There is also a stage/bandstand which is used occasionally. Embarrassingly enough, there was an attempt to get the Lido recognised as the world's shortest pier. It failed.

The Dome

Another iconic structure, this time to the east, is The Dome Cinema - notable for its domed roof unsurprisingly. A feature of many postcards and pamphlets, it might be remembered for its place in the 1987 film 'Wish You Were Here' starring Tom Bell and the lovely Emily Lloyd. In this rather saucy film you will also spot the prom opposite, her fictitious home a few streets away and the shop front of her fathers barber shop in nearby Rowlands Road. Annoyingly, scenes showing beach side iron railings were shot in nearby Brighton.

A little titbit: Emily Lloyd is the daughter of Roger Lloyd-Pack who played Trigger in the TV series 'Only Fools and Horses' also starring David Jason whose brother coincidently lives in Worthing. Emily's mother was a personal assistant to Harold Pinter, playwright, actor and director who also lived in Worthing for a short while. Popular aren't we.

While we're on the subject of films, we might as well blow Worthing's sea shell like trumpet. The 1968 classic film Up the

Junction starring Dennis Waterman, Suzy Kendall and Maureen Lipman, utilised the seafront as part of the backdrop for a planned 'Dirty Weekend' on the coast. For some reason Worthing found favour over near by Brighton.

Back to the Dome. Opened in 1911as an Edwardian entertainment centre called the Kursaal, it featured a roller skating rink complete with an orchestra, an electric theatre upstairs showing early silent films and an outside stage and tea gardens. It was renamed the Dome when WWI closed in as it was thought that the name Kursaal sounded too German - which it was. The man behind it, Carl Seebold, also dropped his middle name which just happened to be Adolf.

The Stagecoach Bus Depot next door also featured in the Emily Lloyd film under the name 'Southdown'. The Dome gardens have long gone and in its place now stands one of the bus sheds which is still known to this day as 'The Gardens'.

The Dome is still a working cinema and events centre for weddings and parties. It is one amongst a few early cinemas in the country that lay claim to be the oldest surviving.

The café next door used to be known as the Rendezvous and was run by Mr. & Mrs. Bonetti the parents of Peter Bonetti the Chelsea & England footballer whose family still reside in the town. It is said that Peter can sometimes be seen in the George and Dragon pub in local Tarring village.

One of the benches on the prom has a small plaque dedicated to the family. In fact, whilst strolling along the seafront we recommend playing 'Spot the bench dedication' game, there are a few to find.

The Prom (West)

The Prom - Tiddy-om-pom-pom. What seaside resort would be complete without one and ours is massive - stretching from one end to the other as they often do. To the west it is sadly quite featureless unless you count public toilets, the odd shelter here and there and rows of iconic beach huts in the far distance interspersed with the occasional fisherman's beach mooring. It is however ideal for jogging, cycling and those romantic strolls into the sunset…if you don't mind dodging the cyclists. Backing the prom are some of our larger hotels including a 'Best Western' and some independents. There is even a bowling alley tucked under the multi-storey car park – one of the local eye-sores. This all eventually fades out to residential housing. Almost at the far end is Marine Gardens, a secluded area featuring a putting green, bowls, garden and café, it almost makes walking to the end worth it.

We are blessed with a sandy beach, - by sandy we mean sand of a larger than average grain size - we call them pebbles.

But when the tide turns a flat plain of grey, sand does appear which is of a more suitable texture, home, we are given to understand, to worms that you are allowed to teach to swim from the pier with a rod and line.

By now you would have worked out the more distant you are from the town centre the more sedate it gets. This aside, summer does bring with it the usual hoards of sun seekers with an abundance of oiled flesh along with children, kite surfers, canoes and jet skis. Deckchairs for hire are a must along with ice cream vans.

Also worth mentioning at this point is the abundance of seaweed that gets thrown up onto the beach each year. At the height of summer, the odour from the rotting mass permeates the air for a fair distance……but at least it masks the smell of the endless traffic and tourist coaches that frequent the seafront at this time of year. Surprised the coaches still come really … perhaps they enjoy playing 'avoid the parking ticket'…but then again, even with the taint of seaweed in the nostrils, Worthing is a far more pleasant environment than even the most fragrant parts of London.

The Prom (East)

East of the pier things are a little different. You have the Dome as mentioned, Steyne Gardens that will be looked at in a moment, as well as Splash Point, cafes, restaurants and other touristy things to delight and amuse.

Bank Holidays will see the inevitable fair ground set up on the esplanade, as well as special events and outdoor shows. To give Worthing its due, it does make an effort to entertain as best it can.

Having now placed you at a suitable point of reference and whetted your appetite we shall fan out and take a more detailed look at the town itself and see what's on offer.

Steyne Gardens

   Set midway between the pier and Splash Point to the east sits The Steyne and its gardens. Flanked by two of its better known hotels and conference centres - the Chatsworth and the Ardington, the gardens are a peaceful retreat for a bite of your Tesco Express sandwich or just a sit down under the shady trees. The word 'gardens' is a bit of a misnomer, being mostly given to grass, however, a small sunken garden at the southern end has been specially designed for those with limited sight as it is planted with scented plant life to lift the senses. In the centre sits a bronze statue, his name is Triton and he's a Greek God. He dribbles water on a good day. At the seafront end of the gardens, in fact, really on the pavement, stands a memorial to those from the town that lost their lives in the Boer War.
   The Steyne is not just a nice place to relax and watch the world go by; it is also a host to special events such as classic car shows, occasional open air pop concerts by local bands...

some of which can actually play, a winter ice rink and the usual charity and Rotary Club events.

Splash Point

At the far end of the prom, or 'Esplanade' as it is sometimes referred to, is Splash Point. A small promontory that's been modernised in a style resembling cubism. Strange blocks of slate jut up inviting bruised knees and cracked heads. Manually operated bursts of misted water add to the effect when it's working. This is modern art apparently. Close by are a couple of cafes and you will find that once away from the town centre, the service goes up and the prices go down.

Splash Point is also the home of our very own Speaker's Corner, although the authors have yet to see or hear any soap box politicians spouting forth.

The north side of the prom is home to smart apartment blocks. What you won't find easily are shops selling Worthing rock, sugared donuts, plastic bucket and spades, flags and the normal beach paraphernalia - a little odd for a seaside town, although these are available at the various kiosks outside the pier. You're not allowed to throw stones at the seagulls either.

If the urge should take you, and we recommend that it should, continue east bound and you'll discover a small artist's enclave known as East Beach Studios where people have done some interesting things with driftwood and paint. Behind this are Denton Gardens, a sheltered walled garden given to flowers and benches. It also boasts a miniature crazy golf course that gives a new meaning to lack-lustre.

One rarity is fresh fish. Here and there when time and tide are right, real fish flavoured fish can be bought from the local fisherman who sell from their beach moorings to passers by. If only we could remember how to cook the things that don't come with instructions on the bottom of a plastic tray.

Town Centre & South Street

Back at the pier and directly opposite heading north is South Street. (Obviously it's heading south if you were at the other end). This is the town centre. Carry on north and it becomes Chapel Road - just to be confusing. South Street used to be the main drag in days of yore, but modern traffic calming in the form of bollards, pinch points and one way systems and not scented candles as we had envisioned, now make it pedestrian friendly - as long as you don't step out in front of a bus.

Being the hub of all things commercial and the terminus for the local buses, it's the place to start and end your journey to and from neighbouring areas such as Broadwater, Durrington, Goring-by-Sea, Tarring, Salvington, West and East Worthing. It is also from here that you can head off in three of the four compass points to enhance your shopping experience.

The Guildbourne Centre

While we're in South Street you will find the Guildbourne Centre. This is Worthing's White Elephant; it is neither white nor an elephant. This brick and concrete structure built in the late 60s replaces three streets, two pubs and probably fifty businesses to bring Worthing kicking and screaming into the realm of the modern shopping centre. It boasts around a dozen active shops.

The upstairs gallery is now deserted and blocked off which is not simply a result of the recent economic downturn but a situation that has blighted the unpopular centre for many years. However, the shops that remain below do make an effort to please, especially the butchers, a rare sight these days. It is also home to Wilkinson's enabling you to pick up some holiday essentials.

Hidden away behind a security door is the faceless local radio station Splash FM. Originally a truly local station and still carrying local interest and advertisements with strong charity support it is now far more commercial than ever and will probably end up absorbed by the likes of the more national Heart FM. Worthing does have one other station the rather dire - Worthing Sunshine Radio - which lacks both direction and sparkle but could be so much more…but at least someone is trying. Meanwhile back outside the Guildbourne centre . . .

To one side of the entrance you might spot Anne Street, home to one of two traditional cobblers in the town. (We'll wait while you younger people look up the definition of cobbler on your smart phone). The centre backs on to another of our expensive multi-story car parks. Note: The gents toilets there are the worst we've ever seen. (Someone take note).

Warwick Street

Off the square from South Street heading east is Warwick Street. A paved pedestrian area thankfully not dominated by the usual big named retail outlets and not a single mobile phone shop in sight. Here you will find a shop that sells local artworks and saucy underwear - an odd combination it has to be said. There are two or three cafes that spill out on to the street giving a delightful continental feel. Also, two good pubs, a music shop and a couple of craft shops should you get the urge for a quick Blue Peter moment.

There is also a Pizza Express tucked away in a little mews. Now we're not singing the praises of a pizza shop, just the building it's in. As strange as it may seem, this was the home for a while of Jane Austin in 1805. It has been said that her unfinished work 'Sandition' was based on Worthing. Sadly there is no pizza based on her. There was one other well known resident but we'll let you look for that Blue Plaque.

The end of Warwick Street merges with the top of the Steyne where even more local business ply their trade. Well worth an explore. Beyond is Beach House Park.

Montague Street

Going back down South Street we find Montague Street off to the west, the biggest, longest and widest paved shopping area in town. Running parallel with the sea front, it has everything you would expect - the well known and unimaginative stores with their everyday one day sales. Come mid-week a market pops up with its folding stalls to thrill you with the usual cheap tat we have come to love. Sadly the street lacks anything really local.

What is worth a look are the side streets. Here, where the small trader has been shouldered away from the limelight are some little gems - cafes, restaurants, craft jewelry, body piecing and even a tattoo shop - go on, give granny a treat.

Keep going and you enter Rowlands Road, a more subdued area, again littered with real shops run by real people, often the ones that own them. It's also the home of the Rose & Crown pub ideal for a pint and a bite away from the hubbub. This end of town is also where you can sample foreign cuisine from the usual Chinese and Indian to Thai, Lebanese and beyond. Home of Worthing's Eastern European contingent, various small supermarkets selling all kinds of strangely named foodstuffs are present.

Oh yes, almost forgot, what every seaside town must have, a bingo hall set in an old cinema. This area is known (or rather promoted by the council) as the West End. Don't expect theatres or shows, it's not *that* West End.

If you want to park illegally, this seems to be the place to go, double parking, pavement parking, you name it this area has it, including a substantial amount of resident only and the usual expensive roadside parking....God knows what would happen should a fire engine need access in an emergency.

Chapel Road

Back in South Street and heading north, we approach St Paul's Church. This imposing four pillared Romanesque building is now better known as Lime Café. Opened in 1812 - the building not the café, it was a Chapel of Ease – from whence the road got its name - for the main church found up the road in Broadwater. These days it's hard to believe a spare chapel had to be built to handle the over-flow. What a lot of sinners we must have been.

Today, business is once again thriving, probably because it's a café. We do drop in for a frothy coffee sometimes and enjoy the surroundings with comfortable sofas, tables and chairs. It's like Christ meets Ikea. St Paul's also holds events from weddings to real ale festivals, club meetings and children's parties. The food isn't the normal fare either, it's not a greasy spoon by a long chalk and you don't have to say grace.

Outside you will find a memorial dedicated to those from the town who perished in WW2.

Diagonally opposite is the main post office where older people try to buy stamps for their emails, bless 'em.

Ambrose Place

Running parallel with the seafront on the south side of St Paul's is Ambrose place. Here is a wonderful collection of gleaming, almost colonial style buildings whose front gardens are oddly on the other side of the road. Once upon a time they had an unhindered view of the sea until the town got in the way and a road cut across their front doors. Still at least you can see who's at the door while you're trimming your bush in the garden.

One of the buildings nearer the far end belonged to the playwright Harold Pinter who we briefly mentioned earlier. One of his plays, 'The Birthday Party', was made into a film and featured a fleeting view of Worthing. There are no prizes for spotting Mr. Pinter's house, the blue plaque gives it away every time.

Opposite Ambrose Place is Union Place heading east. This is home to the Connaught Theatre and the Ritz Digital cinema. Oh almost forgot, yet another over priced car park. Note the theatre's Art Deco styling which we still find very pleasing to this day. Union Place is also home to a rather understated restaurant offering the biggest steaks in town.

Museum & Town Hall

Carrying on northwards up Chapel Road, we find this splendid collection of buildings. The first is the Tourist Information office followed by Worthing's award winning museum. The museum is a must for those interested in history or simply when it's raining. There are many glass cases holding things of local interest - even a skeleton for the children to look at. One section is dedicated to period clothing and is said to include a pair of Queen Victoria's knickers. Imagine trying to find a reason to write that on a post card home! Upstairs, there is a small art gallery which often has themed collections and may or may not have the odd nude.

Behind the Tourist Information office in Richmond Road stands the main library which houses an excellent reference section on the first floor....who knows, one day it may even include a copy of this guide.

The last building in this trio is the Town Hall. The carved inscription on the mantle reads 'Ex terra copiam e mari salutem' or 'From the land plenty and from the sea health', hence the fish and cornucopia on the coat of arms. What a splendid Tesco Express it would make as an addition to the other nine in the town (bit of a dig there).

Just past the Town Hall is a war memorial dedicated to those from the town that fell during World War One

In Stoke Abbot Road on the northern side of the town hall stands the Assembly Hall complex - another popular venue with the Worthing Symphony Orchestra, Europe's largest organ (a Wurlitzer apparently) and visited by many touring bands.

A smaller hall attached, The Richmond Rooms, can be a self supporting venue or part of the Assembly Hall complex. Ideal for stamp collectors fairs as long as no-one opens the windows.

Teville Gate Shopping Centre

Traipsing further north, we discover even more of the little shops so easily bypassed on our way to town and then we hit Teville Gate. Named after the Teville stream that stills runs underground, this now desolate area was once a 1960s shopping centre. Sadly no-one used it and it fell into decline, eventually demolished to make way for these gleaming glass apartment blocks rivaling the great London Gurkin itself, a multiplex cinema, new restaurants and coffee shops with beautiful landscaped public areas….at least that's the plan. What a good impression it makes as people enter the gateway to the town. As you can see, it's in full swing (Not).

One thing in its favour is the car park which has a £3 a day parking offer and there is a Park and Ride scheme operated in summer. Just don't leave your car there after dark.

Worthing Station

This is Worthing Station - one of three in the town, the others being West Worthing and East Worthing. This is the point of arrival for many travelers. It's a fifteen minute walk to the town centre or sea front and is served by the local buses and taxi service. Note that buses stopping directly outside the station are heading into town where as the buses stopping short on the approach are heading out of town. It gives one, or at least us, a twisted kind of pleasure to see the look on people's faces as they depart heavily laden with suitcases for places unexpected (to them anyway).

A short walk around the block you'll find local shops for local people - but they're still happy to see you.

Sadly, the station is not the best of places to be in the evening. It tends to be a magnet for youths not quite old enough to get in to the club opposite. That, coupled with the late night kebab bars means it can get a bit messy.

Beach House Park

Back in the town centre and heading east along Warwick Street, we exit the street and carry on past the Steyne. As the shops start to peter out and you pass Warwick Place, notable for the unique boat arch door ways, you come upon Beach House Park on the left and Beach House itself on the right.

This well maintained park plays host to the annual World Bowls Championships with five superbly kept greens, three tennis courts and an excellent café - if it hasn't been burnt down again. A little known feature is a rock garden dedicated to some dead pigeons. We could tell you why but that would spoil the fun of you finding out. For those 'of an age' Nancy Price had a hand in it.

There are also two outside garden chess boards set in tarmac - not the normal sort of course, this is the large garden version. Sadly we've found no clue of who to ask for the playing pieces and presumably a wheelbarrow or two to carry them in.

It is useful to know, that across the road at the top end of the park is Worthing Hospital - just in case you do your back in playing chess. It also has a car park, the usual exorbitant charges apply.

Beach House

Beach House itself is a rather lovely regency style villa that was home to the rich and famous - the picture above is the southern aspect by the way. You have probably cottoned on to the fact that that it has become separated from the gardens by the busy Brighton Road.

To drop some names of former residents, we have Sir Frederick Roe, head of the Bow Street Runners, Sir Edmund Loder and his friend King Edward the VII who stayed for a sleep over a couple of times, and Edward Knoblock, playwright, whose guests included JB Priestly.

The grounds to the south include public tennis courts, beach volley ball complete with sand and if you're very lucky, semi-naked people playing it.

At the time of writing, a new swimming pool is being constructed to replace the existing one called the Aquarena and is to be named 'Splash Point' - not to be confused with Splash Point which is a short stroll away ....don't ask! Just up the road is a rather ugly block of flats featuring a disused petrol station below, this was where Oscar Wilde wrote 'The Importance of Being Ernest'. It wasn't flats then.

High Street

Unlike most high streets that run through the centre of town, ours doesn't, that would be too logical – well actually, it used to be the main street until focus shifted to the aforementioned South Street. As Worthing became more civilised and discovered the joys of a sewerage system, large villas and town houses tended to be constructed with a leaning to the west away from the labouring class, thus leaving the old High Street somewhat isolated. Today it boasts a multi-storey car park, a Waitrose supermarket, a Lidl if Waitrose poses too much of a financial commitment, one café, some empty shops (at the time of writing) and the Job Centre.

At the northern end is The Stage pub. We must be careful to say that this is a gay friendly pub, not a gay pub. We have visited on a couple of occasions (curious but not curious if you know what we mean) with no worries about dropping coins on the floor.

Diagonally across the road is The Swan pub. Much more of a traditional place all round with occasional folk music evenings and the odd bit of poetry thrown in. Good old British stuff.

Parking

Not a hope. Worthing is famed for the high parking charges in its multi-stories and on street parking fares little better. Local residential parking is permit only and supermarkets check your length of stay. The multi-storey in Teville Gate does an all day ticket for £3 which in daylight hours is fine but one wouldn't leave a car there after dark. Not a positive point …. get a bus in.

Eating

Fast food here is in abundance, as are cafes and fish and chip shops - you name it we've got it. There is also a fine selection of restaurants with real cutlery too. Tempting as it is to name some of the better ones we will hold back incase: A) they change owners and get worse or B) they change owners and get better.

Drinking

The town centre pubs during the day are welcoming but evenings and weekends are best left to the younger generation. This is the time when bouncers try to keep trouble makers out and the police try to keep them in.

Don't get us wrong, in the early evening you'll stare in wonder at the delights of young ladies wearing next to nothing - even in the depths of winter. Themed fancy dress nights often add an amusing quality. But take a walk there early the next morning and you'll be stepping over half eaten kebabs, burgers and vomit. Credit to the council who are quick to clear up this mess and return the town to normal.

We personally make a b-line for the pubs on the periphery or tucked up back streets well off the beaten track.

Again we withhold naming names (even though we have) because there's only so much free beer we can drink.

Broadwater

North of the town centre lies Broadwater. Like many large towns Worthing absorbed its nearby villages. Oddly, Broadwater village existed before Worthing and was the controlling parish, Worthing was then little more than a few fishing shacks. It still remains a little distant and has its own personality. About half-way along the road to Broadwater you will find the Manor Sports Ground, home to Worthing Cricket team.

In the 'village' itself, there are about fifty shops, a large green with a cricket pitch and pavilion. Four pubs, the Cricketers, and the Broadwater are prominent but The Old House At Home and The Elms are tucked away to the east.

Now this may sound a little odd, but a visit to Broadwater Cemetery is recommended, preferably while you're still upright. During summer months regular themed tours are held by local historians revealing fascinating facts and amusing anecdotes about our long time dead.

West Worthing

West Worthing was built some time back as a separate entity in its own right, but has over ensuing years become amalgamated into the connurbation that Worthing has become.

Getting here is easy as it is on the same main rail route as Worthing central station. Unfortunately, it is the rail crossing that makes the area somewhere to avoid if you want to simply pass through, as when the barrier comes down and you are caught within its grasp, you have no choice but to sit and wait for a train to pass.

Not so bad you may think, the British enjoy queuing, but sitting there as you watch train after train appear and disappear without knowing whether the barriers will rise or another train is due can seem like an eternity.

As if to tease, the barrier will often rise raising expectations as you slowly creep forward two car lengths before the barriers come down again for an indeterminate time to heighten levels of frustration. The crossings even had their own Twitter account for a while.

On a positive note, there is plenty of free on street parking and you will find few if any regular high street names with most being small independent concerns including a good old fashioned butchers shop, a green grocers and a rather excellent stationary shop....unless of course it has moved. It also boasts a pub right opposite the station, a café or two, burger bars, an excellent Indian restaurant and numerous other fast food outlets...useful when camping in the queue to cross the rail line.

The best way to avoid the endless waiting is to take the train or walk from the town centre some 20 minutes away. Alternatively, you could visit during off peak times, but then all the shops are shut making it a rather pointless exercise as there is nothing of note to see.

To the north, the road will take you up another South Street, past more small shops to Tarring village. To the west, is Goring-by-Sea.

Another shopping 'centre' exists a ten minute walk south west of the station, offering more familiar names, including the ubiquitous Tesco Express, Iceland, Boots the chemist and a Co-op as well as some more independents and a smattering of charity shops and fast food outlets…it is worth checking out the Indian restaurant here too.

If you find yourself hankering for a pint whilst about here, you can pop into the local hostelry adjacent to the roundabout…..just don't expect an intimate local feel, being a 'family' pub, you'll find more atmosphere on the moon.

West Worthing does have one landmark, known it seems only to a few locals. Grand Avenue, is exactly what it says on the tin, a wide part tree lined avenue that heads southwards down to the sea. It was at one time bedecked on both sides by large detached dwellings, but sadly many of these houses have now disappeared to be replaced by modern blocks of flats.

In days gone by, Grand Avenue was known as Ladies Mile opposite the south end of which was to be the location of Worthing's second pier. Regrettably, the plan never came to fruition, but on the road side of the promenade directly opposite Grand Avenue can be found what was to be part of the entrance to the planned pier in the shape of an ornate wall and pillars, that without knowledge of the proposed development seem slightly out of place.

East Worthing

Trying desperately to think of something flattering about east Worthing - nope not working. Truth be known, the one real land mark was the Half Brick pub on the sea front. A sign to all Worthingites that they were once again approaching home.

Forced to close because no one could afford the ever spiraling breweries prices, it signaled the end for a building that was twice washed away in storms. (It was eventually moved inland a tad when they realized the beach wasn't the best place for a pub.) Now it is currently being converted into apartments. The original frontage remains due to its Grade Two listed status.

The pub derived its name from what it was constructed with – half bricks. To its east, large brickfields were dug harvesting the clay for local construction and the original pub was probably built for the workers out of the broken and split reject bricks.

It was to be discovered that a band of clay with an odd blue tinge near the foreshore was when fired, producing a fine yellow brick that became popular and can still be spotted in the town to this day.

A little further on and spanning the boundary between Worthing and its neighbour Lancing, is Brooklands. Originally called Brookfields, this is where the Teville stream emerges and joined forces with the sea and is consequently prone to flooding…never mind, we don't like Lancing anyway.

Massaged over time, it became what it is today, a pleasure park with a boating lake, pitch & putt and a children's play area. Best not forget the miniature railway and café.
Other than that, East Worthing has little to offer the casual visitor. Two small parades of shops, a couple of pubs and three industrial estates, home to the likes of GlaxoSmithKline (formally Beechams) and B&W, both large employers of Worthing labour.

Tarring

Tarring covers a large area but the heart lies very much in the old village north of West Worthing. One of the first places you'll notice is the pub, the George and Dragon in the High Street. Possibly dating back to 1658 when it was the White Horse. A look up the high street itself will reveal its provenance. Old half-timbered buildings can still be spotted especially the Parsonage Restaurant which is a fine example. Another excellent pub, well it was…although still has a great garden, can also be found nearby.

Across the road is the Archbishops palace founded in 1250. Don't expect something grand, it's not, but it is remarkable that anything still remains. It is now part of a school.

A little way down the road heading south is the Old Fig Garden dating back to 1785. Sadly, it's no longer the size it used to be due to housing development but many old fig trees still remain. It is said that they were planted by Thomas A Becket but no proof has ever come to light to say he ever visited. The garden (now private property) is open for just one day a year.

Durrington

It might be a little harsh to say that Durrington isn't really of interest but it just isn't. This is very much a residential area. There's a couple of pubs and open spaces but little of note other than the odd flint cottage.

Salvington

Salvington gets a mention because of its windmill. As you've guessed, it's on top of a hill and not the easiest place to get to. Dating back to 1750, it is a restored working post mill open to the public at certain times. One of the authors admits that he once attended a tour and came away with a new respect for the miller and his wife especially when finding out she had to turn the mill around to face the wind.

Goring-by-Sea

Sounds rather posh doesn't it. Shouldering on the western edge of Worthing it is mainly residential with a couple of small local shopping parades.

Close to Durrington-on-Sea station (it is called that to differentiate it from Durrington station situated elsewhere in the country - in fact, Durrington-on-Sea station is really in Goring-by-Sea….Goring-by-Sea station is further west….) stands Field Place. Today it is a sort of recreation centre set around an 18th century manor house and has its own resident ghost. There are indoor and outdoor bowling greens (you've noticed our obsession with bowls by now. If Worthing had a traditional costume it would be bowling whites and a flat cap), four netball courts which double as tennis courts – or is it the other way round? pétanque – look it up we had to, putting and table tennis. This compliments the Leisure Centre on the other side of the railway line.

Talking of railway lines, Field Place is also home to a model railway, not a tiny one like the one your dad has in the loft, this is the bigger 'ride on' version with real steam and operates on occasional summer weekends.

An old barn on the site was a few years ago converted into a theatre which also doubles as a function room and is available for hire.

As a point of interest to those keen on government institutions, just south of the station at Durrington lies the Inland Revenue Offices. Nothing to see really, so no need to tax yourself getting there. An interesting fact though, is that during World War Two, the site was an RAF hospital.

Another landmark, just north of the station, is the old Lloyds Bank building. Built in the 70s, it had a huge digital clock on the south and north sides that could be seen from some distance away - no excuses for local employees to be late for work then. However, the clock was always prone to breaking down and has now not been working for some years, but the external 'faces' have never been removed.

The seafront offers a large green area for sporting activities along the lines of kite flying and kite surfing. The sea front café is popular and recommended. Apparently Peter Townsend of The Who recorded beach sounds for the bands album Quadrophenia here.

Highdown Hotel and Hill

Not easy to get to this one but well worth the effort. Highdown was a manor house set in a rather unique garden and it's this garden that is its main feature. First of all it's free, and there are tea rooms and the manor house hotel in case you don't want to leave. The gardens make up a whopping eight and a half acres - not that we really know how big an acre is. The plants and trees form part of a rare collection from around the world that has managed to survive on this chalk hill side.

The building used to be home to Stern's nightclub during the 80s when rave culture was de rigueur. Its success as a rave venue eventually became its downfall due to the associated drug taking and dealing that the movement attracted.

It was, incidentally, named Stern's after the family that originally owned the house.

Just behind and above the house is Highdown Hill, an old hill-fort complete with Saxon burials and the famous Miller's tomb. Well worth a walk on a summers day giving an excellent panoramic view of the town and coastal plain.

Day trips

One thing Worthing is good for is being used as a base from which to go exploring.

Brighton is some 12 miles to the east. It is of course a city and has everything you'd expect from such. One drawback is getting there. The road from the north is more or less a straight line and takes you directly to the seafront but unless you know where you're going, finding a parking place can be a bind. The roads from the east and west offer similar frustrations. The seafront route offers the additional joy of road clogging traffic and endless traffic lights with associated annoyances. The road from the south is well……er…wet!

The trains from Worthing station are regular and frequent and plonk you directly into Brighton station. The city centre is a simple downhill walk and starts outside the station door.

The 700 Coastliner bus service operates a fifteen minute service to Brighton city centre from Worthing seafront and stops in Churchill Square, the main shopping centre, and then on to Brighton Pavilion before coming back. Just remember on the return journey to get off or you'll end up in Portsmouth.

Arundel is one of our favorite places. A wonderful town giving more than just a nod to its history. The castle is a must but the admission fee is expensive. You can spend hours looking around the local shops and sampling cream teas sitting by the river. Driving there involves a major road and taking the correct junction off. Parking again is difficult as Arundel by its very medieval nature is cramped. Yes there is a station, but it's just outside town and you'll have a fifteen minute walk crossing a busy road. Again, a 700 Coastliner bus serves the town - just make sure it says Arundel on the front. It is confusing as there are two 700 services, but basically every third one goes only as far as Arundel via Littlehampton.

Littlehampton is a popular place to visit, probably because its name sounds like a joke from a carry on film. We suppose it is itself a seaside resort like Worthing. It certainly has the typical family holiday feel with beach side amusements, parks, a small shopping centre and a river. Driving is again a matter of following the signs. Littlehampton is a train terminus, thus not every coast line train goes there. It's best to wait for a direct link as changing can get you lost. The 700 Coastliner bus service pops up again - all 700s go to Littlehampton.

Further a field still lies Chichester, Bognor Regis, Horsham, Crawley, Petworth and Midhurst to name just a few.

Places to stay

We're not short of accommodation that's for sure. Hotels are in abundance and offer all the normal things like running water and fresh hay. But we would recommend perhaps looking at the bigger arena of bed and breakfast for that more homely touch. A wide collection nestle on the seafront just a ten minute walk along the seafront in the east as shown above.

Camping is a problem; Worthing doesn't really cater for it. There is a Caravan Club site on the outskirts but pitching a tent locally can't be done.

Youth Hostels. Nope.

Did You Know . . .

Worthing was host to many a musical phenomenon Jimmy Hendrix, The Who, David Bowie, Pink Floyd and Motorhead to name a few. The Pavillion Theatre has for many years been on the circuit for the plethora of stand up comics – Jim Davidson, Alan Carr, Ken Dodd and so forth.

We have a pillar box with the insignia of King Edward the VIII who abdicated before becoming King. It's still in active service because no-one realizes its significance.

Broadwater Green used to have a ducking stool. Not for drowning witches as many would like to believe, but was instead used as a form of punishment for local misdemeanors and spreading gossip - probably why they are usually depicted with women tied in the seat. The intention was not to drown but to humiliate.

Arthur Conan Doyle, the creator of Sherlock Holmes, popped down to Worthing to open a spiritualist Church in Grafton Road. There is a small plaque outside.

Detective Inspector Walter Dew the man who caught Crippen retired from the police and settled in Beaumont Road in Worthing. His small bungalow was called 'The Wee Hoose' but was renamed 'Dew Cottage in 2005 in his honour. Walter is buried in Durrington Cemetery.

Crippen's murdered wife Cora Crippen was buried in St Pancras Cemetery, London. The marble headstone was made by Councillor Francis Tate at the Stonemasons workshop in North Street, Worthing.

If you're into telephone boxes - and who isn't? A K8 (Kiosk – Design 8) can be found on private property but in public view in Park Road opposite the hospital. It is said that only 12 of these boxes remain operational.

I was Monty's Double. Yes it was a film and a true story to boot. Meyrick Clifton James was an actor and by all accounts not a particularly gifted one. However, he did have a stunning resemblance to Field Marshal 'Monty' Montgomery. Spotted by David Niven who was working for the war office, Meyrick was to become Monty's official double. Playing his new role he would tour England and abroad giving rousing speeches to the military. He retired to Worthing where he wrote the book 'I Was Monty's Double' that was later to become a popular film starring John Mills. Meyrick starred in the film as himself.

St Mary's Church in Broadwater was host to a secret Cliff Richard Concert. Not quite what you would expect, it was just him, a guitar and gospel songs. This can be verified by one of the authors as he literality bumped into him.

Roy Orbison was a regular visitor too, not to perfrom but to visit a friend who had a small business here.

Goring Hall, now a private hospital, was once a school and was attended by a young Bob Monkhouse during the war. His parents decided he was safer on the coast than in London. Bob's memoirs recall how he witnessed a dog fight resulting in the German plane crashing.

Winston Churchill was given the freedom of the borough in 1947 but declined because he couldn't spare the time to visit and pick it up. He did however visit in 1958 to watch a play at the Connaught Theatre featuring his daughter Sarah. The play was 'Variation' by Terence Rattigan. No-one knows if he popped into the Town Hall to collect his freedom?

Alma Cogan was brought up in Worthing and started her career singing with a band on the pier. She went on to become Britain's highest paid singer in the 60s

Worthing produces its own independent monthly history and social comment magazine called the Worthing Journal available in selected shops displaying their poster. More should follow suit.

Keith Emerson of the prog rock group Emerson, Lake and Palmer was raised in the town.

The once named William Broad – better known as Billy Idol was also a one time resident as was the Radio 2 DJ Simon Mayo, journalist and broadcaster Derek Jameson, actress Pauline Collins, actor Hugh Lloyd, Bob Monkhouse, Harold Pinter, Jane Austen,….and so it goes on.

Katie Price – to some better known as Jordan has a house in Goring.

Worthing is twinned with…

Elzach, Germany

Gutach im Breisgau, Germany

Les Sables-d'Olonne, France

Simonswald, Germany

Waldkirch, Germany

At a Glance

Theatres

Pavillion Theatre – Marine Parade, BN11 3PX, 01903 206206
Connaught Theatre – Union Place, BN11 1LG, 01903 206206
Northbrook Theatre – Littlehampton Road, BN12 6NU, 01903 606162
Assembly Hall – Stoke Abbot Road, BN11 1LG, 01903 206206

Cinemas

Ritz Digital Cinema – Union Place, BN11 1LG, 01903 206206
The Dome – Marine Parade, BN11 3PT, 01903 823112

Sports Centres and 'stadiums'

Worthing Leisure Centre – Shaftesbury Avenue, BN12 4ET, 01903 502237
Davison Leisure Centre – Selbourne Road, BN11 2JX, 01903 204668
David Lloyd Centre – Romany Road, 0845 1252 782
Field Place – The Boulevard, BN13 1NP, 01903 244034

Worthing Football Club – Woodside Road, BN14 7HQ, 01903 239575
Worthing Rugby Club – Roundstone Lane. Angmering, BN16 4AX, 01903 784706
Worthing Thunder (basketball) - see Worthing Leisure Centre
Worthing Cricket Club – Broadwater Road, BN14 9DT, 01903 238329

Swimming Baths

The Aquarena – Brighton Road, BN11 2EN, 01903 231797

Golf Courses

Worthing Golf Course – Links Road, BN14 9QZ, 01903
260801
Hill Barn – Hill Barn Lane, BN14 9QF, 01903 237301
Ham Manor - West Drive. Angmering, BN16 4JE, 01903
783288
Rustington Golf Centre – Golfers Lane, Angmering, BN16
4NB, 01903 850790

Car Parks

Leave the car at home, hitch-hike, get a cab or bus, walk
even.....

Links

Worthing's own website: www.visitworthing.co.uk
Worthing Town Centre: www.worthingtowncentre.co.uk
Dome Cinema stuff: www.worthingdome.com
Pier: www.piers.org.uk/pierpages/NPSworthing.html
Lido: www.theworthinglido.co.uk
Museum & Art: www.worthingmuseum.co.uk
Salvington Mill: www.highsalvingtonwindmill.co.uk
Highdown Gardens: www.highdowngardens.co.uk
Worthing leisure: www.worthingleisure.co.uk
Worthing Theatres: www.worthingtheatres.co.uk
St Paul's: www.limecafe.co.uk/cafes/st-pauls
Broadwater Cemetery: www.fbwc.co.uk
Pubs & their history: www.worthingpubs.com
WSR: www.worthingsunshineradio.com
Splash FM: www.splashfm.com
Worthing Journal: www.worthingjournal.co.uk
Worthing Herald: www.worthingherald.co.uk
Wikipedia: http://en.wikipedia.org/wiki/Worthing
Live Camera: www.worthingseafront.co.uk

Parking & Prices: http://en.parkopedia.co.uk
A great searchable car parking finder for the UK

Searchable map:
http://www.yell.com/ucs/UcsSearchAction.do?
view=map&location=worthing-west+sussex

Trip Advisor: www.tripadvisor.co.uk/LocalMaps-g190761-
Worthing-Area.html

Downloadable PDF of bus routes:
www.stagecoachbus.com/PdfUploads/**Map_24_01%20(Worth
ing).pdf**

In conclusion

Car parking is perhaps the biggest hindrance to tourism being overly expensive and restrictive. The general area still carries the image as a retirement home. Youth entertainment is limited thus making it over subscribed. Worthing seems to lack that true 'kiss-me-quick' seaside resort image. Lacks colour and lustre.

On the plus side, the staged shows are good if a little dated. A wide variety of cuisine to please most palettes is on offer. It's by the sea. Has a good local transport system and access to a main line rail station. Good pedestrian areas for safe and easy shopping. Knotted hankies on the head are acceptable. Sea front cycle hire in season. Caters well for the disabled. Good open spaces. Has a mildly amusing guide book. Open Sundays.

Don't think for a moment that this simple guide sums up Worthing - we've barely scratched the surface. We could for instance tell you why the pasty shop in South Street looks like the back end of a galleon, (did you notice the man in a barrel above it?) or perhaps the airmen who sacrificed their lives by crashing into the sea. Or even the bag lady shepherding around five heavily laden supermarket trolleys. Everything has its story, its reason to be and only living here will afford the benefit of true knowledge. We've given you a taster of its sweet and sour!

James Henry & Colin Walton

You Can Stop Now

You can stop reading now; this is the back of the book where it gets boring.

All details are to our knowledge correct at the time of publishing. So if you get lost or a building has mysteriously disappeared it's because we've erred or you didn't get the joke.

Written by James Henry & Colin Walton
Published October 2012
Picture Credits & Cover: James Henry
Beach House: Pete Brant
Editing & Proofing: Colin Walton
Special mention: Nope, We think we've over played our part.

Other books by Colin Walton: pending
Other books by James Henry:
'Driver, do you stop at the station?'

Printed versions of these books are available from Lulu.
http://www.lulu.com/gb

Printed in Great Britain
by Amazon

64529996R00034